IMAGES
of America

PITTSBURGH'S
IMMIGRANTS

"Home is just the place where I eat and sleep. I live in the mills," said one unidentified steelworker. The telling quote was featured in Stefan Lorant's book, *Pittsburgh: The Story of an American City*, forth edition. This photograph *Iron & Steel* by Ross Altwater captures the essence of Pittsburgh in the late 19th and early 20th centuries. (Carnegie Library of Pittsburgh.)

On the cover: A steelworkers' English class began at the YMCA in Lawrenceville in 1913. Please see page 65. (Carnegie Library of Pittsburgh.)

IMAGES
of America

PITTSBURGH'S
IMMIGRANTS

Lisa A. Alzo
with the Carnegie Library of Pittsburgh

ARCADIA
PUBLISHING

Published by Arcadia Publishing
Charleston, South Carolina

Library of Congress Catalog Card Number: 2006921065

For all general information contact Arcadia Publishing at:
Telephone 843-853-2070
Fax 843-853-0044
E-mail sales@arcadiapublishing.com
For customer service and orders:
Toll-Free 1-888-313-2665

Visit us on the Internet at www.arcadiapublishing.com

To my grandparents, John Alzo and Elizabeth Fenscak Alzo,
and John Figlar and Verona Straka Figlar—your courage, determination
and faith brought you to America and provided me with
all of the opportunities I enjoy today.
This book is for you.

CONTENTS

ACKNOWLEDGMENTS

I would like to thank all of those who made this book possible through their donation of historic photographs, especially Gregory Lazarchik, John Matviya, Teresa Sinchak, and the countless individuals (too numerous to list by name) who captured the essence of Pittsburgh's immigrants on film and donated their personal or professional photographs to the Carnegie Library of Pittsburgh. In addition, I extend a deep appreciation to the photographers and historians—Ross Altwater, Frank E. Bingaman, Clyde Hare, Stefan Lorant, Luke Swank, and anyone else I may have inadvertently overlooked—who photographed the faces and places of western Pennsylvania, and documented the various immigrant cultures, events (both the day-to-day and the memorable) in all of Pittsburgh's neighborhoods.

I am deeply grateful to the staff at the Carnegie Library of Pittsburgh, especially Marilyn Holt, Gladys Maharam, Sheila Jackson, and Gilbert Pietrzak for opening up their doors and photographic library to me and for their careful and dedicated assistance throughout the planning of this book, and to the Pittsburgh Custom Darkroom for their photographic services.

I also wish to thank my editor at Arcadia Publishing, Erin Vosgien, for her expert guidance and for patiently and cheerfully answering all of my questions during the editorial process.

To my grandparents, John Alzo and Elizabeth Fenscak Alzo, and John Figlar and Verona Straka Figlar, for having the courage to "get on the boats" and sail to a new life in America, and for passing on your dedication to family, deep faith, and strong work ethic to your children and grandchildren. This book is for you and the countless number of other immigrants who chose to call Pittsburgh home.

Finally, to my husband, Michael, a big thank you for your constant encouragement and support, for always pushing me to do my best, and for your immeasurable patience in dealing with the many moods and temperaments of a writer in search of her creative muse.

INTRODUCTION

"Gateway to the West," "Steel City," "City at the Point," "City of Champions." For the past several decades, the city of Pittsburgh, Pennsylvania, has donned many monikers reflective of its geographic features, its industrial and manufacturing history, and the success of its many professional sports teams.

Yet, the essence of this great American city is not defined by the height of the buildings that shape its dramatic skyline, the natural confluence of its famous three rivers, or its prominence as a major industrial center. The heart and soul of this great American city comes from its people.

Since the mid-1700s, Pittsburgh has welcomed generations of immigrants. This region in southwestern Pennsylvania was once a magnet for European immigrants who carved out livings in the steel mills, iron, glass, and other factories along its three famous rivers. Those immigrants built the city's ethnic neighborhoods—the German North Side, the Polish South Side, the Italian Bloomfield, the Irish of Upper Lawrenceville as well as other immigrant enclaves in smaller cities and towns in the surrounding areas. The diversity of Pittsburgh's neighborhoods symbolizes a city truly rich in history and culture. Many notable Pittsburghers in business, the arts and entertainment, and sports were either immigrants themselves or children of immigrants.

While other major cities in America also attracted their share of immigrants, there is just something about Pittsburgh. Perhaps author Jonathan Yardley put it best in his 1993 book, *States of Mind: A Personal Journey Through the Mid-Atlantic*: "By then I had concluded that Pittsburgh was the friendliest of cities, hiding its financial and industrial might behind the good manners and modest style of ordinary America at its best."

In reviewing images for this book, I found it a difficult task to choose from the seemingly unlimited number of historical photographs available. While it was not possible to include all of the wonderful images of immigrants that came my way, I attempted to select those that best represented the key immigrant groups and prominent neighborhoods of Pittsburgh from the late 18th century through the mid-20th century.

Pittsburgh's Immigrants pays tribute to the hardworking men and women who made significant contributions to the growth and development of western Pennsylvania and left a legacy of rich and vibrant ethnic culture that endures to the present day.

One

ARRIVAL

Western Pennsylvania (defined as the 26 counties west of State College Pennsylvania) has played a significant role in the development of the United States. Pittsburgh is by far the commonwealth's largest city out west. Even before America's Revolution, the confluence of the Allegheny, Monongahela, and Ohio Rivers (later referred to as the "Point") was critical to the settlement and growth of Pittsburgh. Since colonial times these rivers transported Americans and the nearby land provided food. The area's plentiful natural resources provided energy, heat, and shelter for early settlers, while its industries—glass, iron, and steel—offered employment.

Dubbed "Gateway to the West," Pittsburgh became the logical stopping place for many pioneers migrating to Ohio, Indiana, Illinois, and points further west. With this westward migration, Pittsburgh became a vital link in trade and communication between the eastern cities, the Ohio and Mississippi Valleys, and the Great Lakes region. The expense of shipping goods over the mountains and the ease of shipping down river to western markets encouraged Pittsburgh to become more self-sufficient in manufacturing goods for its own use and for trade.

As Pittsburgh grew, so did its surrounding towns.

Taken from the south side of the Monongahela River, the first sketch of Pittsburgh was drawn in 1790 by Louis Brantz, a Philadelphia merchant, who wrote that "the view from this spot is in truth the most beautiful I ever beheld." Brantz's original is now in the Carnegie Library. Seth Eastman redrew the original for Henry R. Schoolcraft's *Respecting the History, Present Condition and Future Prospects of the Indian Tribes of the United States* of 1847. (Carnegie Library of Pittsburgh.)

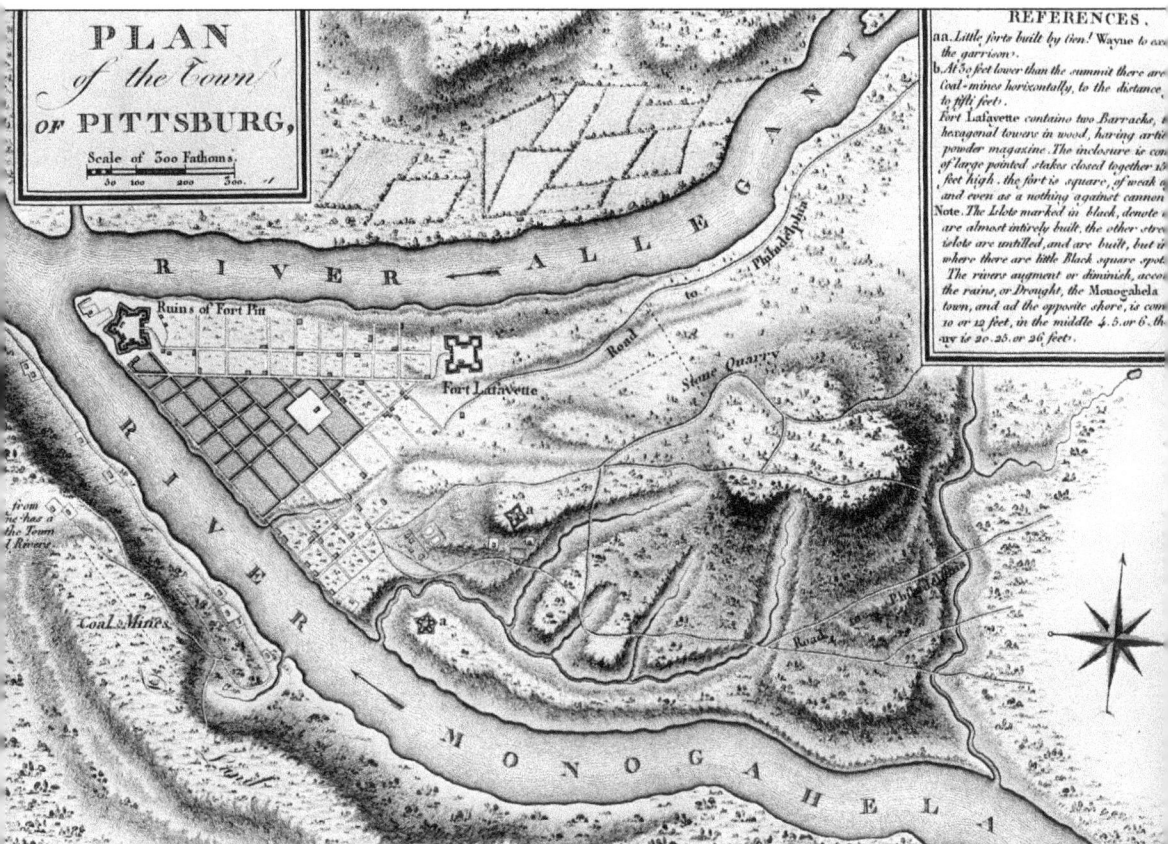

This plan of the town of "Pittsburg" was made in 1826. The drawing includes markings for coal mines, as well as the famed "three rivers"—the Allegany, the Monongahela and the Ohio, and other noted historic sites such as Fort Lafayette, and the Ruins of Fort Pitt. Pittsburgh was incorporated as a city by an act of legislature on March 18, 1816. Through a printer's error, the "h" was omitted from the name, but the original charter included it. Unfortunately the original was burned when the second Allegheny County Court House was destroyed by fire in 1882. Consonant with the rise of the modern technological age, a gradual tendency toward standardization appeared. In accordance with this trend, the United States Board of Geographic Names was appointed in an effort to standardize the orthography of American place names. Pittsburgh officially lost its "h" when the board's report was approved by Pres. Benjamin Harrison on December 23, 1891, until July 19, 1911, when at a special meeting of the United States Geographic Board, the previous decision was reconsidered and the "h" was to be reinstated. (Carnegie Library of Pittsburgh.)

Rivers served as the main arteries for commerce in the latter part of the 18th century, and from the outset, Pittsburgh was a key city. Produce was loaded onto flatboats, like the one pictured, and sent down the Ohio River. An average trip to Louisville and back took approximately three months. In addition to the transport of agricultural produce, flatboats, keelboats, and barges also carried many immigrants and their possessions westward to new lands. (Carnegie Library of Pittsburgh.)

This is a drawing of Braddock's Field in 1803. Gen. Edward Braddock, in command of the British expedition against Fort Duquesne, was defeated by the French and Native Americans on July 9, 1755, in what are now the boroughs of Braddock and North Braddock. The fighting took place as the French and Native Americans formed a semicircle about the British, who were massed on a line that extended from about the site of Copeland Station on the Pennsylvania Railroad to a point on the river not far from the mouth of Turtle Creek. The worst confusion and the greatest part of the slaughter were near what are now Jones Avenue and Bell Avenue, to which point the British advance had been driven back. After two hours of fighting, in which about 500 British were killed, and Gen. Braddock was mortally wounded, the British retreated and crossed the Monongahela River at what is now the Edgar Thomson Steel Works. (Carnegie Library of Pittsburgh.)

This is a view of the city of Pittsburgh in 1817. (Carnegie Library of Pittsburgh.)

Seen here is Pittsburgh, as seen from Coal Hill (Mount Washington) around 1850. It is from an original steel engraving by a German, Edouard Willman, who died in 1877. (Carnegie Library of Pittsburgh.)

At one time, lumbering was a chief industry in Pennsylvania. This picture shows a typical lumber camp near Penfield around 1884. (Carnegie Library of Pittsburgh.)

Taken at Mix Run in 1897, this is a telltale remembrance of what once occurred in the timber country of western Pennsylvania. At that time, the state led the country in production of timber. The picture appeared in the *Pittsburgh Sun-Telegraph*, Color-Gravure Section, on January 11, 1932. (Carnegie Library of Pittsburgh.)

The Old Eagle Cotton Mill in Allegheny is seen her, built in the days when canal boats were used. This drawing was copied from *Palmer's Pictorial Pittsburgh* by R. M. Palmer, Pittsburgh, 1905. (Carnegie Library of Pittsburgh.)

Salt, required to preserve meat, was a precious commodity. In 1790, one barrel of salt was worth 20 barrels of wheat. Salt was transported from the east by packhorse, and later, by boat from Kentucky. Around 1800, a major industry developed in Pittsburgh from the discovery of salt in the Conemaugh Valley. This image from an oil painting by W. T. Russell Smith, dated 1832–1834, depicts the salt works on Saw Mill Run. (Carnegie Library of Pittsburgh.)

Two

The "Steel City"

The Steel City
I'm Pittsburgh, the city of iron and steel,
The city of crucible forge and mill;
The mines of the world my treasury is;
The forces of earth is slave to my will.

—"Song of Pittsburgh"
George H. Thurston, 1886

In Stefan Lorant's book, *Pittsburgh: The Story of An American City*, Sylvester K. Stevens wrote: "For the building of railroads, of cities, of factories, America needed iron and it needed steel."

Seven large steel works in Pittsburgh made 30,000 tons of steel in 1870. Five years later the Edgar Thompson Works in Braddock began to use the Bessemer converter under the supervision of ironmaster, Bill Jones, heralding the "era of steel." Within a decade, the industry employed some 8,100 workers and Pittsburgh's steel production was valued at $18,300,000; capital had increased to $12,000,000.

"And as Pittsburgh was the center of iron and steel production, the city became the hearth of the nation."

PITTSBURGH
FLINT GLASS MANUFACTORY,
Corner of Grant and Water Streets.

BAKEWELLS & CO.

DESTROYED BY BIG FIRE, 1845.

Benjamin Bakewell came from England in 1808 to start a factory that became widely known for its fine cut flint glass. This illustration of Pittsburgh Flint Glass Manufactory, on the corner of Grant and Water Streets comes from George T. Fleming's *Views of Old Pittsburgh: A Portfolio of the Past*, edited by Henry Russell Miller, 1932. (Carnegie Library of Pittsburgh.)

Henry Bessemer, an English iron man patented a method in 1855 whereby carbon and other impurities are removed from the molten pig iron. The Bessemer process made steel manufacturing cheaper and more efficient. This drawing, by C. S. Reinhart in *Harper's Weekly* on February 18, 1871, depicts *Melting Steel*. (Carnegie Library of Pittsburgh.)

18

In 1863, Henry W. Oliver, William J. Lewis, and John Phillips began to manufacture nuts and bolts. Lewis, the inventor of a bolt-heading machine, sold out his interest in 1880 to the Oliver brothers and Phillips. This photograph copied from *A Pittsburgh Album*, 1959, shows how their South Side operation at Eleventh and Muriel Streets looked in 1887—a year before it was organized as Oliver Iron and Steel Company. To the right, a neighboring house with white laundry hanging in the yard provides a stark contrast to this industrial image. (Carnegie Library of Pittsburgh.)

The old Smithfield Street covered bridge, built in 1818 and destroyed by fire in 1845, is featured in this picture of the Monongahela Wharf painted by Leander McCandless Esq. around 1825. Several houses are also shown including from left to right the Mansion of Gen. William Wilkins, the political power in Pennsylvania, secretary of war, minister to Denmark and Russia, this house served as a stop where General Lafayette, General Jackson, General Taylor, Daniel Webster, Henry Clay, Calhoun, Benton and all the notables passing through Pittsburgh were entertained; the old woolen mill, later the site of the first free school in Pittsburgh, later becoming the old south or second ward but occupied at the time of this painting by Monongahela House; the Irwin's Tavern, a famous old hotel where people from the east stopped when going south and west; the Anderson's mansion; and the Bakewell's Glass House. On the river are the pirogues, a craft used by river men which was poled by hand. A high sand bar in the Monongahela River had a crop of rye raised on it in 1825. (Carnegie Library of Pittsburgh.)

This c. 1900 photograph by Harry B. Johnston shows Pittsburgh's Grant Street. The church pictured in the foreground is St. Peter's Episcopal (dismantled in 1901 and reassembled on Forbes Street in Oakland). The church in the background is St. Paul's Cathedral. (Carnegie Library of Pittsburgh.)

This scene of Liberty Avenue and Grant Street in 1913 was captured from the Pennsylvania Railroad Station. The old Lafayette Hotel is the white building on the corner. (Carnegie Library of Pittsburgh.)

A photograph, dated February 1, 1927, from the Department of Public Works shows the Forbes Street curb looking east from Murray Avenue. Several stores including a cigar shop, luncheonette, and a plumber can be seen. (Carnegie Library of Pittsburgh.)

A busy day on Fourth Avenue is seen here. It was once known as the "Wall Street of Pittsburgh," because it was home to many of the financial institutions that fueled the industrial revolution. (Carnegie Library of Pittsburgh.)

VIEW N.WEST - FROM ROOF OF UNION STATION
FROM A POINT ON NORTH SIDE OF BUILDING AT
EXTREME WEST END.
WEATHER CLOUDY - WIND FROM SOUTH EAS
JUNE 20 1906. 11:35 A.M. N°.2765

This picture shows a smoggy view towards the Strip District taken June 20, 1906. When the steel mills were at full throttle in Pittsburgh, the air was so thick with pollution from factory smokestacks that the city turned streetlights on during the daytime. (Carnegie Library of Pittsburgh.)

This *c.* 1900 view is of the Carnegie Steel Company's Painter's Mill located on Pittsburgh's South Side. Near the mills was "Painter's Row," where the company housed certain of its employees, mostly immigrants. (Carnegie Library of Pittsburgh.)

Seen here is another view of the Painter's Mill. This photograph shows the bar and sheet plant, which covered a large area on the South Side below the Point Bridge. In the background is Duquesne Heights. (Carnegie Library of Pittsburgh.)

Dubbed "Gateway to the West," Pittsburgh became the logical stopping place for many pioneers migrating to Ohio, Indiana, Illinois, and other destinations further west. This scene of the Pittsburgh Wharf was taken on October 18, 1929, when the completion of construction work on the lock and dam system in the Ohio River was celebrated by a marine parade. In the foreground is a Jones and Laughlin tow, consisting of coal barges and car ferry barges, on the way from the Pittsburgh works on the Monongahela River to the Aliquippa works on the Ohio River. (Carnegie Library of Pittsburgh.)

Three

WHERE THEY WENT

The majority of the early immigrants in western Pennsylvania were Scotch-Irish, German, English, French Huguenot, and Swiss. In the 1870s, the region attracted large numbers of immigrants from southern and eastern Europe. These included Slavs, Poles, Italians, Jews, Russians, and Greeks seeking the promise of a better life.

During the 19th and especially the 20th centuries, blacks from the southern states also moved to Pennsylvania in large numbers. Between 1870 and 1900, Pittsburgh grew into a classic melting pot.

Pittsburgh's cultural diversity is still reflected in its many ethnic neighborhoods that tell their stories with food, customs, and cultural celebrations. Many of these ethnic neighborhoods are shown in the photographs on the following pages.

This photograph, taken by Clyde Hare in 1950, shows an overall view of Pittsburgh's North Side. The North Side, a patchwork of smaller neighborhoods, was itself once a city, now nostalgically remembered as "Old Allegheny." Annexed by the City of Pittsburgh in 1907, the city of Allegheny was once the fashionable home of some of western Pennsylvania's wealthiest families. (Carnegie Library of Pittsburgh.)

Here is a view of Valley Street on Pittsburgh's North Side. This area is lined with streets full of historic homes and beautiful architecture. Despite redevelopment, the North Side remains a place of great charm, beauty, and vitality. (Carnegie Library of Pittsburgh.)

This photograph shows a view of buildings No. 3101 to 3119 Carson Street on Pittsburgh's South Side in 1932. The South Side was once composed of a number of smaller communities including Birmingham and East Birmingham. Birmingham quickly became a sizable industrial center because of easy river transport and abundant coal supplies. The South Side produced a number of major Pittsburgh businessmen. The South Side business district was a once-thriving marketplace. The area closest to the river, called "the Flats," was home to the industries—glass, iron, and steel—that provided much of that famed heat. The factories' employees, many of them immigrants from eastern Europe, built small houses for themselves on the South Side's "slopes," the hillside that rose above the industrial area. (Carnegie Library of Pittsburgh.)

The Hill District borders downtown to the east and stretches along Centre, Forbes, and Fifth Avenues to the edge of Oakland. It is surrounded by Oakland, the Strip District, and Polish Hill. After the Civil War, mirroring the changes in America at large, wave after wave of ethnic groups made the Hill their home, coexisting side by side, lending to the neighborhood's rich cultural history. (Carnegie Library of Pittsburgh.)

The Hill is a gallery of faces full of character, strength, and tenderness. It is the poetry of language captured in the plays of August Wilson. It is the daily lives chronicled in Robert L. Vann's crusading *Pittsburgh Courier*. A center that drew musical genius, it was also the site of Greenlee Field where once the legendary Pittsburgh Crawfords battled the equally legendary Homestead Grays in celebrated Fourth of July ball games. In this 1930 photograph, some shoppers pose in front of a store. (Carnegie Library of Pittsburgh.)

Another *c.* 1930 photograph of the Hill District shows the Gorton's Codfish building with a man looking out from an upstairs window. Since the 1940s and 1950s, urban planners pursuing a vision have redeveloped the Hill, but it still survives with a spirit that can never be lost. (Carnegie Library of Pittsburgh.)

In this undated photograph, folks gather for a Sunday afternoon church service in the Hill District. (Carnegie Library of Pittsburgh.)

Squirrel Hill is one of Pittsburgh's premier residential neighborhoods. The area was first settled in the 18th century as a pioneer farming community. As the city of Pittsburgh prospered, so did the status of Squirrel Hill. In 1867, Squirrel Hill was incorporated into Pittsburgh, but large portions of the neighborhood remained as farmland or large country estates into the early 20th century. The neighborhood's primary era of growth was from 1900 to 1930, due in part to the connection of the Boulevard of Allies to downtown. During this time, Squirrel Hill developed into a lively center of Jewish life, with Jewish restaurants, kosher shops, and bookstores. This photograph shows an aerial view of Squirrel Hill in the mid-1950s. (Carnegie Library of Pittsburgh.)

Bloomfield, located just east of downtown Pittsburgh, is surrounded by the Pittsburgh neighborhoods of Shadyside, Friendship, Garfield, Lawrenceville, and Oakland. Bloomfield's name was derived from the many wild flowers that bloomed there years ago. In the late 1800s, mill workers in nearby Lawrenceville constructed small row houses designed for single families and businesses in the style of their homeland. Today, well-maintained row homes along quaint, narrow streets characterize Bloomfield. Here homes are often passed down through families, and grandchildren usually live just a few blocks from grandparents, aunts, uncles, and cousins. This photograph shows housing in the Juniper Street area of Bloomfield. (Carnegie Library of Pittsburgh.)

The contrasting images of a motor car alongside a horse-drawn carriage are shown side-by-side in this c. 1950 photograph of a street scene in the Bloomfield area. (Carnegie Library of Pittsburgh.)

Around the time of the American Revolution, the area now known as East Liberty was a free grazing area in Allegheny County located near the eastern edge of the town then known as Pittsburg. Alexander Negley's son Jacob Negley married Barbara Winebiddle, built a manor house, and developed a village that he called East Liberty after the old grazing commons. In 1816, Jacob saw to it that the Pittsburgh-Greensburg turnpike was built through East Liberty, which made the area a trading center and ensured its future growth. East Liberty truly began to develop as a commercial area in 1843, when Jacob's daughter Sarah Jane Negley married the ambitious lawyer Thomas Mellon, who worked to make East Liberty a transportation hub—Mellon convinced some of Pittsburgh's first trolley lines to pass through East Liberty. In 1868, the City of Pittsburgh annexed what is now East Liberty. Thanks to its favorable location and Mellon's guiding hand, it became a thriving commercial center in the following years. East Liberty's merchants served many of Pittsburgh's industrial millionaires, who settled in nearby Shadyside and Point Breeze, as well as professionals in Highland Park and Friendship and laborers in Bloomfield and Garfield. By 1950, it was a bustling and fully urban marketplace, and was in fact the third-busiest retail center in Pennsylvania, behind only center city Philadelphia and downtown Pittsburgh. (Carnegie Library of Pittsburgh.)

This is a picture of Garden Street and the H. J. Heinz plant taken in 1952. In 1896, Henry Heinz turned more than 60 products into "57 Varieties." The magic number became world-renowned and now is virtually synonymous with the H. J. Heinz Company. (Carnegie Library of Pittsburgh.)

The borough of McKees Rocks lies along the west bank of the Ohio River, adjoining Pittsburgh. It was known for its extensive iron and steel interests, as well as large railroad machine shops, and various manufactories. In 1900, 6,353 people resided in McKees Rocks. The borough derives its name from Alexander McKee, to whom a 1,300 acre tract of land was given in 1764, and from a rocky projection into the river at this place, which can be seen in this undated photograph. (Carnegie Library of Pittsburgh.)

This c. 1916 photograph shows workers outside the employment office building at the Pressed Steel Car Company in McKees Rocks. (Carnegie Library of Pittsburgh.)

Here is an illustration that shows a parade along an exuberant Eighth Avenue in Homestead, around 1900. In less than 30 years, the number of residents had spread from the original six houses to reached a total of 25,000 in Greater Homestead. When the photograph was taken in 1946, Greater Homestead had 60,000 people. The paved street prevented marchers from getting stuck in the mud. (Carnegie Library of Pittsburgh.)

Located just 11 miles southeast of Pittsburgh, Duquesne was once primarily an area of fertile farmland. A steel mill was first built in Duquesne in 1886. Two companies failed to make a go of it. Andrew Carnegie, who introduced large-scale steelmaking into the region a decade earlier at the Edgar Thomson Works in nearby Braddock, took over the facility in 1891. Between 1893 and 1901 Carnegie transformed the Duquesne Works into a fully integrated basic steel plant. Financier J. P. Morgan, owner of National Tube Works, a finishing-steel company, offered to buy Carnegie out, along with other steelmakers. Carnegie agreed, for $492 million in 1901, and United States Steel—the world's first $1 billion corporation—was born. This photograph shows the Duquesne furnaces in 1906. The Duquesne Works was once one of the largest and most advanced steelmaking operations in the world. (Rotograph Company.)

Four

FAMOUS FACES

The value of Pittsburgh's three rivers, as well as its growing self-sufficiency, was not lost on early industrialists who also served as some of the city's earliest philanthropists who would provide funding for the libraries and other cultural institutions that are still so vital to the area today.

Among the moguls was Andrew Carnegie, a young executive of the Pennsylvania Railroad, who noticed the heavy wear and tear on the iron train rails that often caused train derailments. Building on his knowledge that the railroad was ordering Bessemer steel rails from England, Carnegie decided to quit his railroad job to manufacture these rails in Pittsburgh, and in 1875 opened the Edgar Thomson works at Braddock for the production of cheap, high-volume steel in the Pittsburgh region. Soon other plants followed in nearby Duquesne, McKeesport, Homestead, and other towns.

Following Carnegie's lead, industrialists such as Henry Clay Frick, Henry John Heinz, and Andrew Mellon, among others, built their fortunes in Pittsburgh. This chapter includes images of some of the influential names that played key roles in Pittsburgh's development, along with a few common folk who gained notoriety at the local or national level.

William Pitt, the elder (1708–1778), was the man for whom Pittsburgh was named. Pitt was the earl of Chatham and the brilliant, aggressive prime minister of England who came to power in 1757. His war leadership resulted in British victories both in Europe and the French and Indian War. This image is from a copy of the original painting. (Carnegie Library of Pittsburgh.)

William Pitt, the younger (1759–1806) was painted by Edward Francis Burney. He was the son of the elder Pitt, and at age 24, became England's youngest ever prime minister, and served as one of the longest in the role (18 years, 343 days). This photograph is of a painting in the Chancellor's Office at the University of Pittsburgh. (Carnegie Library of Pittsburgh.)

The man who named Pittsburgh was Gen. John Forbes (1707–1759). Forbes commanded the British expedition against Fort Duquesne. (Carnegie Library of Pittsburgh.)

This is a picture of Henry Bouquet (1719–1765), the Swiss professional soldier who came to the New World in the spring of 1756, and served under General Forbes on his campaign against Fort Duquesne. (Carnegie Library of Pittsburgh.)

This illustration comes from Palmer's Prominent Pittsburghers, R. M. Palmer 1905. From left to right are (first row) Gen. J. Wilkins Jr., Andrew Watson, Oliver Ormsby, and Isaac Ferrer; (second row) Harmar Denny, James Ross, Walter Forward, and Gen. James O'Hara; (third row) Hon. William Pitt, Col. Henry Bouquet, Gen. Edward Braddock, and Capt. M. De Beujeu. (Carnegie Library of Pittsburgh.)

The parents of composer Stephen Collins Foster are William Barclay Foster and Eliza Clayland Tomlinson Foster. They are shown in this undated portrait. William Barclay Foster was the third mayor of Allegheny City. (Carnegie Library of Pittsburgh.)

Stephen Collins Foster was born in Pittsburgh on the Fourth of July in 1826—the ninth child of a well-to-do family. He showed his talent at a young age and became known as "the creator of the first distinctively American musical idiom, the singer of the commonplace, the elemental, and the democratic." During his life he wrote more than 200 songs—many of which are still recognizable today, including, "Oh! Susannah," "My Old Kentucky Home," and "Jeanie with the Light Brown Hair." Although a successful composer, Foster's earnings were small and financial problems plagued him until his death in 1864. When he died, he had in his pocket 38¢ and a scrap of paper with the words "Dear Friends and Gentle Hearts." (Carnegie Library of Pittsburgh.)

Capt. Edward W. H. Schenley was the British army officer whose third elopement was with Pittsburgh heiress Mary Croghan. He was 43 and she was 15. His two earlier wives had died. While Schenley Park bears his name, he was never more than a visitor. (Carnegie Library of Pittsburgh.)

Perhaps one of Pittsburgh's most famous immigrants, Andrew Carnegie is shown here in this portrait by B. L. H. Dabbs. Andrew Carnegie was born on November 25, 1835, in Dunfermline, Scotland. He was just a boy of 13 when he came to the United States with his parents in 1848 from Glasgow, Scotland. Carnegie worked as a bobbin boy in the cotton mill, the career that led him into railroading and steel, and eventually to a millionaire's fortune. He is quoted as saying: "Pittsburgh entered the core of my heart when I was a boy, and cannot be torn out. I can never be one hair's breadth less loyal to her, or less anxious to help her in any way, than I have been since I could help anything. My treasure is still with you, and how best to serve Pittsburgh is the question which recurs to me almost every day of my life." Carnegie died on August 11, 1919 in Lenox, Massachusetts, and is buried in Sleepy Hollow Cemetery in North Tarrytown, New York. During his lifetime, Carnegie distributed $350 million for philanthropic purposes, and left a substantial amount for further distribution after his death. (Carnegie Library of Pittsburgh.)

Henry Clay Frick (1849–1919) was a superb business organizer and genius in management who began his career at a young age. While keeping books in the distillery of his grandfather Abraham Overholt, he started to operate coke ovens in the surrounding coal district. By the time he was 30, Frick was a millionaire. Andrew Carnegie's mills were Frick's largest customers, and at age 41, he became the head of the world's greatest steel and coke operation, employing 30,000 men. In later years, Frick and Carnegie became enemies. So much so, that as the story goes, on a spring day in 1919, when a dying Carnegie sent a letter to Frick to propose a final meeting after two decades of separation, Frick replied, "Tell him I'll see him in Hell, where we are both going." (Carnegie Library of Pittsburgh.)

Richard King Mellon (1899–1970) began his Mellon Bank career as a messenger, and rose to president in 1934 at age 35. From his father he learned to "live where you work and work where you live." (Carnegie Library of Pittsburgh.)

This photograph shows a very regal looking Richard K. Mellon on horseback in June 1929. (Carnegie Library of Pittsburgh.)

Andrew William Mellon (1855–1937) was a financial genius who left his mark on Pittsburgh by helping the development of its major industries. He became head of T. Mellon and Sons Bank in 1880. From it, he and his brother Richard B. Mellon, with combined interests in coal, coke, steel, aluminum, oil, and so on, developed one of the world's greatest financial empires around the Mellon National Bank, incorporated in 1902. After serving 11 years as secretary of the U.S. Treasury, Mellon was named ambassador to England in 1932. Following his death in 1937 at age 82, estimates of his public bequests were as high as $500 million dollars. This photograph is a copy from an oil painting by Oswald Birley. (Carnegie Library of Pittsburgh.)

46

From a horseradish patch he planted in 1869 on his farm in Sharpsburg, Henry J. Heinz, who came from German stock, built a multi-million dollar food business that eventually included ketchup, celery sauce, pickled cucumbers, sauerkraut, and vinegar, among other products. At his death in 1919, Henry was succeeded by his sons Howard (president) and Clifford (vice-president). Henry is seen in this c. 1904 photograph, with son Clifford, taken at his Penn Avenue Mansion. (Carnegie Library of Pittsburgh.)

Henry Phipps (1839–1930) was Andrew Carnegie's business associate right from the start. In 1867, Phipps, Carnegie, and others formed the Union Iron Mills. Phipps had a legendary reputation for close trading and was known as an "eagle-eyed manager," watching over accounts, costs and production methods, and suggesting improvements and economies. (Carnegie Library of Pittsburgh.)

The Honorable William Wilkins (1779–1865), was the son of Capt. John Wilkins Sr. (1733–1809), and a prominent Pittsburgh jurist, president of the Bank of Pittsburgh, United States senator, secretary of war under President Taylor, and United States minister to Russia in 1834–1835. In 1839, he constructed a stately mansion called Homewood. He died on June 23, 1865, and is interred in Homewood Cemetery in Wilkinsburg—a town named for him. (Carnegie Library of Pittsburgh.)

This photograph is a portrait of Matilda Dallas Wilkins (the second wife of Hon. William Wilkins) and her daughter Henrietta C. Wilkins. Matilda was born in 1798, the daughter of Alexander James Dallas, a prominent Philadelphia attorney, and secretary of the treasury under President Madison. Matilda became the founder of Calvary Episcopal Church when she convened a meeting of East Liberty residents in Louis Castner's drug store in January 1855. (Carnegie Library of Pittsburgh.)

Alice Longworth (center) was the daughter of Theodore Roosevelt and a descendant of Nicholas Roosevelt, who built and launched, in Pittsburgh in 1811, the *New Orleans*, the first steamboat to travel western waters. (Carnegie Library of Pittsburgh.)

Arthur J. (Art) Rooney (1901–1988) (left) was born in Coultersville, east of Pittsburgh. He is quoted as saying, "My mother's people were all coal miners and my father's people were all steel workers," and while growing up he lived with his family on the second floor of his father's bar, Dan Rooney's saloon in Pittsburgh. The founder of the Pittsburgh Steelers, Rooney funded the purchase of his football franchise in 1932 by a win on the horses. In this undated photograph, Art Rooney is shown with Jockey Eddie Arcaro. (Carnegie Library of Pittsburgh.)

Women voted for the first time in Pittsburgh in 1920. Jennie Roessing, pictured here, was a top leader (along with her friend Hannah J. Patterson) in local and national suffragist movements. To gain support for the woman's vote, she drove a Liberty Bell truck over rural roads of the state. (Carnegie Library of Pittsburgh.)

Elizabeth Jane Cochrane (1864–1922), known as "Nellie Bly," was a newspaper reporter for the *Pittsburgh Dispatch*, where she reported on factories and public institutions and wrote about the theater, on art, and on society. She took the name from Stephen Foster's song "Nelly Bly, Nelly Bly! Bring the broom along." In 1887, Nellie Bly left Pittsburgh for New York, and in 1890, at age 22, she completed a trip around the world in 72 days that made her a celebrity. (Carnegie Library of Pittsburgh.)

Five

DAILY LIFE

For decades, the feeling of security that resulted from living among people who spoke the same language and had the same cultural or religious background provided the glue that has traditionally bonded ethnic communities together.

Seeking to keep their culture as it existed in the homeland, immigrant groups frequently founded their own churches, schools, boarding houses, and other institutions, as well as forming their own academic, athletic, or charitable groups, and fraternal, occupational, and social organizations. Many also established their own ethnic presses that published newspapers and histories to highlight specific communities.

The photographs that follow offer a brief glimpse into what daily life was like for some of Pittsburgh's immigrants. As will be seen, the quality of life varied depending on social status, and was almost as diverse as the immigrant groups themselves.

This photograph, from the family album of George Lipman, shows a dapper Pittsburgher as he looked in the 1880s. (Carnegie Library of Pittsburgh.)

Here is an example of what a "well-dressed child" in Pittsburgh looked like in 1906. This photograph of a Wilkinsburg boy in his Sunday best appeared in the Gravure Section of the *Pittsburgh Sun-Telegraph* newspaper on March 15, 1931. (Carnegie Library of Pittsburgh.)

This picture depicting "The Days of the Narrow Waist," was taken around 1888 on a lane above the Ohio River leading to French Point, at Economy, now Ambridge. Shown from left to right are Libbie Buckles, Stella Feucht, and Anna Feucht Woods. (Carnegie Library of Pittsburgh.)

A well-dressed woman poses in this photograph in the gay 1880s in her panniered skirt, basque of plaid taffeta, high collar, and bustle. Her curled bangs add to the impeccable style. (Carnegie Library of Pittsburgh.)

L. E. Carmack, of 724 Orchard Avenue in Bellvue, looks quite stylish for a 12 year old in this undated photograph, as she demonstrates "What the Young Girl used to Wear." (Carnegie Library of Pittsburgh.)

This photograph illustrates how fashions changed, even in the early 20th century! It required a lot of tailoring to dress up the girls in 1904, but smart effects were achieved with no sacrifice in the matter of warmth in winter styles. (Carnegie Library of Pittsburgh.)

The first sheath dress in Pittsburgh, worn by an unidentified woman, is shown in this June 1908 picture. (Carnegie Library of Pittsburgh.)

In this 1910 photograph, D. K. Bryson, Elizabeth Strickler, and Carrie Johansen pose in stylish millinery. When this photograph appeared in the *Pittsburgh Sun-Telegraph* on May 17, 1931, Strickler was approaching her 94th birthday. (Carnegie Library of Pittsburgh.)

This photograph of Mr. and Mrs. R. M. Beatty of Carolyn Avenue in Bellvue, illustrates what the well-dressed honeymooners wore in 1912. (Carnegie Library of Pittsburgh.)

This photograph showing "Hoop Skirts of Old," was preserved by Anita Mae Lintak of Farrell to illustrate the type of dresses her grandmother used to wear. It first appeared in the *Pittsburgh Sun-Telegraph*, Color-Gravure Section, on February 21, 1932. (Carnegie Library of Pittsburgh.)

Pupils at the Alinda Preparatory School, located at North Craig Street and Fifth Avenue, enjoy some time outside in this 1898 photograph. (Carnegie Library of Pittsburgh.)

Pittsburghers battle the elements with umbrellas as they make their way down the concourse in front of the Pennsylvania Station on a rainy day in Pittsburgh around 1907. (Carnegie Library of Pittsburgh.)

Streetcars were once a popular form of transportation in Pittsburgh. This photograph, taken July 6, 1925, shows people boarding streetcars on Smithfield Street and Fourth Avenue. (Carnegie Library of Pittsburgh.)

A young African American girl is standing on a step in a street scene near Woods Run. (Carnegie Library of Pittsburgh.)

Two unidentified young girls from the Soho District of Pittsburgh pose in this *c.* 1900 photograph. The *Gazette Times* sign is seen in the background. (Carnegie Library of Pittsburgh.)

This 1930 photograph offers a view of Pittsburgh's Mount Washington blanketed with snow. Although a pretty scene, Pittsburgh's many hills and bridges could became quite treacherous to travel in the winter. (Carnegie Library of Pittsburgh.)

High-necked waists, long skirts, and long hair proved the fashion of the day for these students in the Margaret Morrison Carnegie School for Women in its first year. This photograph appeared in the *Pittsburgh Sun-Telegraph*, Color-Gravure Section, on November 23, 1930. (Carnegie Library of Pittsburgh.)

Members of the Ladies Guild of St. Marys Byzantine Catholic Church in Bradenville pose in this 1918 photograph. The church was founded in 1905 to serve the needs of more than 100 Russian immigrants from Saris County Slovakia and their families who settled in this coal-mining community located in Westmoreland County, approximately 35 miles from Pittsburgh. (Gregory Lazarchik.)

A group of unidentified African American immigrants pose at an unknown location for this *c.* 1900 photograph. (Carnegie Library of Pittsburgh.)

This photograph, which appeared in the *Pittsburgh Survey* of 1907–1908, shows immigrants in Basin Alley in the Italian quarter on the Hill in Pittsburgh. The *Pittsburgh Survey* serves as the exemplar for the social survey. Most likely influenced by Charles Booth's *Life and Labour of the People in London* (1902–1904) and Jane Addams's, and others, *Hull House Maps and Papers* of 1895, the survey was a project of the journal *Charities and the Commons*, and was directed by Paul Underwood Kellogg. The intention for the survey was to improve life in Pittsburgh as well as to provide a model for intervention in other urban center. Initial funding was by the Russell Sage Foundation, and a massive undertaking was organized. In 1907, Pittsburgh was the fifth largest city in the country and had experienced rapid industrial growth and massive immigration. The city was particularly interesting to the researchers because of the perception that industrialization had been so rapid that living and working conditions could not keep pace. Progressive reforms taking place in other American cities were hindered in Pittsburgh by the oppressive power of both the industrialists and the political machine. (Carnegie Library of Pittsburgh.)

Greek immigrants Louis and George Diacopoulos, Louis Schooles, and Louis Sarris take a break from enjoying some food and drink to pose for this undated photograph. Most Greeks immigrated to Pittsburgh between the years of 1930 and 1960. (Carnegie Library of Pittsburgh.)

Thirteen Hungarian refugees pose in this undated photograph. Many circumstances brought Hungarians to America, and particularly to the Pittsburgh and suburban areas. At the beginning of the 20th century, America needed muscle power to work in mines and factories as well as on railroads. Of note, in the Pittsburgh area, cigar manufacturing was prevalent. At one time there were 235 cigar factories in Pittsburgh, which hired Hungarians, and especially Hungarian Jews who were proficient in Hebrew as well as Hungarian. (Carnegie Library of Pittsburgh.)

This photograph from the *Pittsburgh Post* on November 23, 1902, shows "The Thanksgiving Turkey from 'Foundry' to Oven"—workers picking and dressing turkeys in a Pittsburgh poultry dealer's establishment. (Carnegie Library of Pittsburgh.)

Another holiday photograph portrays "Christmas in the Coke Country—Foreign Cokeworker Ready for a Rabbit Hunt—His Family in Holiday Raiment." The image is from a photograph by I. F. Bole of Scottdale, Pennsylvania, and copied from the *Pittsburgh Bulletin* from December 23, 1899. (Carnegie Library of Pittsburgh.)

An unidentified man plays the accordion while other household members look on in this photograph taken by Lewis W. Hine at the Russian boarding house, Homestead Court, in the spring of 1908. (Carnegie Library of Pittsburgh.)

This photograph, which shows a bustling Saturday night on Saloon Corner in Homestead, was taken by Hine and included in the book, *Homestead: The Households of a Mill Town* by Margaret F. Byington. (Carnegie Library of Pittsburgh.)

Many immigrant steelworkers attended mill-sponsored English classes to help them learn the language and assimilate into America. This photograph shows a steelworkers' English class that began at the YMCA in Lawrenceville in 1913. A large sheet of paper is shown to the left with printed phrases, which begin with "I awake from sleep. I open my eyes. I look for my watch." They end with "I put on my vest and coat. I open the door of my bedroom, I go down the stairs." This simple phrasing assisted the newcomers from Europe who often found it difficult to master the English language. (Carnegie Library of Pittsburgh.)

"They were pouring in by thousands," reflected the steel man in Marcia Davenport's 1942 novel, *The Valley of Decision*, "almost swamping the market at slow times, helping to turn out phenomenal quantities of steel when business swung upwards, their sweated wages undercutting the hard-fought scale of the Amalgamated and all the old-established Irish and Scotch and native men. They held no skilled jobs." This photograph of Slavic mill workers at a Homestead boarding house, around 1909, was taken by Lewis W. Hine, whose interpretative photographs of the good and evil around him are among the finest social documents on record. "Hunky" was the descriptive name given to a foreigner or immigrant laborer, first made popular in Pennsylvania when singling out Hungarian, Lithuanian, and Slavic workers. Hunky was often interchanged with "Bohunk," formed from two other words: Bohemian and Hungarian. Hine's photograph appeared with many others in the *Pittsburgh Survey*, published in 1910, by the Russell Sage Foundation. This six-volume work, the most comprehensive sociological study ever made in this country to that time, helped bring about social reforms both here and in other large cities. (Carnegie Library of Pittsburgh.)

This *c.* 1915 photograph shows a group of men and women—many carrying baskets—waiting in a Depression bread line. (Carnegie Library of Pittsburgh.)

The effects of the Great Depression (1929–1939) were widespread. Those who found themselves without work came in all sizes and nationalities. By 1932, U.S. manufacturing output had fallen to 54 percent of its 1929 level, and unemployment had risen to between 12 and 15 million workers, or 25 to 30 percent of the work force. This photograph documents the plight of a long line of unemployed Pittsburgh men on their way to the capital. (Carnegie Library of Pittsburgh.)

Washing clothes was typically an all-day event. In this undated photograph, an unidentified woman finishes hanging several shirts on a line outside of her home. In the heydays of the steel mills in Pittsburgh, it was commonplace to see women scrambling to gather their clean clothes and bring them into the house before the mills let out the soot and dirt from their smokestacks. (Carnegie Library of Pittsburgh.)

Sometimes immigrants married outside of their own circles. This was the case with the Matviya family seen in this photograph. Standing from left to right are Mary Matviya (née Kocis), Mickey, John, Michael, Andy Jr., Mary and Andy Sr. Michael was the only son to marry another Slovak. Mary's husband was Slavic but the others married into English/Irish families. John married a woman who was from English/Irish stock and was born in Duquesne Pennsylvania, but moved a few miles from Bairdstown when she was a young girl. (John Matviya.)

Members of the Polish fraternal organization G.P. 154 Zwiazek Narodowy Polski (ZNP), founded in the year 1890, are pictured celebrating their 40th anniversary in 1930. This photograph was taken before they had their building at Freyburg and South Eleventh Streets. (Carnegie Library of Pittsburgh.)

This undated photograph shows the celebration of a real Polish wedding. The bride's elaborate headdress is distinctly noticeable. A large gathering of wedding guests, dressed in native costume, watch as the bride and groom join hands during the ceremony. (Carnegie Library of Pittsburgh.)

Seen here is a typical Slovak immigrant couple on their wedding day. Note the traditional dress of the bride. This photograph of Janos Alsio and Erzebet (Elizabeth) Fencak was taken on January 21, 1915. Janos (who later changed his name to John Alzo) was born January 1, 1894, in Kucin, Hungary (later Slovakia), and arrived at Ellis Island on October 29, 1910. Erzebet was born on February 10, 1897, in Posa, Hungary (later Slovakia), and arrived at Ellis Island on May 14, 1914. (Lisa A. Alzo.)

Another Slovak couple, Andrew and Susan Harman, pose on their wedding day in 1914 in Homestead. Notice the similarities in the wedding dress shown in the previous photograph. (Teresa Sinchak.)

Memorial photography was a popular way to honor the deceased in the late 19th and early 20th centuries. This family photograph of Duquesne resident Michael Sivak was taken at the time of his burial in 1919. Behind Sivak are, from left to right, John Alzo, Elizabeth Fenscak Alzo holding baby Anna, Andy Sivak, Martin Straka, Rev. John Szabo (pastor of Saints Peter and Paul Greek Catholic Church), Andrew Hleba (church cantor), Mary Straka Sivak, John Kolcun, Mike Sivak, and Michael Straka. (Lisa A. Alzo.)

Six

AT WORK

When one thinks of Pittsburgh, the association is the "Steel City." But Pittsburgh was more than just steel. Actually, the production of wooden kegs and barrels and glass manufacturing predated its iron and steel mills. And workers in Pittsburgh's many factories made electrical equipment, generators, and turbines. They also packaged food, built fine carriages, and turned out aluminum utensils and cork products. The city also had its share of bankers, businessmen, grocers, and shopkeepers.

Men, women, and children labored for their wages, and also worked in their homes. Pittsburgh's immigrants were doers.

This pictorial drawing is of one the first stores in Pittsburgh, if not the first. (Carnegie Library of Pittsburgh.)

Pittsburgh's first department store, known as Perkins' in 1836, was an old landmark. The store stood at Third Avenue and Market Street, where Thomas Perkins, a jeweler, and John Hammond, a shoemaker, conducted business. A picture gallery was conducted on the second floor. (Carnegie Library of Pittsburgh.)

This butter, eggs, and cheese commission house was located at 205 Wood Street in 1887. In this photograph, taken by Frank Bingaman, are, from left to right, M. F. Breitweiser, Garibaldi McFudd, Frank Colman, B. L. Greitweiser (seated), and two unidentified boys. (Carnegie Library of Pittsburgh.)

Several men show off their fine suits in front of J. F. Maeder's tailoring in this photograph, taken around 1890. (Carnegie Library of Pittsburgh.)

This photograph shows a shopper selecting a piece of produce at a grocery store in the Hill District around 1930. (Carnegie Library of Pittsburgh.)

Two women engage in conversation in front of a grocery store in this 1930s photograph. (Carnegie Library of Pittsburgh.)

This undated photograph shows several men standing in front of F. Baxmyer and Company grocery store on Pittsburgh's South Side. (Carnegie Library of Pittsburgh.)

An unidentified woman passes by this Confectionery Store in Pittsburgh around 1930. Notice the ice box on the outside and the "Rooms for Rent" signs in the windows. (Carnegie Library of Pittsburgh.)

The DeRoy Brothers had been in business some 35 years before this photograph was taken in the early 1880s. (Carnegie Library of Pittsburgh.)

Several people pose outside of Steuernagel Brothers hardware, located on East Ohio Street, in this 1896 photograph. (Carnegie Library of Pittsburgh.)

Several chickens were photographed in the window of a poultry store in Pittsburgh's Hill District around 1930. (Carnegie Library of Pittsburgh.)

Workers are shown stacking produce in this undated photograph taken at a South Side grocery store. (Carnegie Library of Pittsburgh.)

A man poses outside of Murphy's five-and-ten cent store in this undated photograph. The store's slogan, "Nothing Over 10¢," is boldly painted above the door frame. This first Murphy store with its windows full of festoons of lace and rolls of wall-paper was in McKeesport. Walter C. Shaw and John S. Mack purchased the business in 1911, and the G. C. Murphy and Company grew from a small regional operation to the third largest variety store chain in America in volume of business. (Carnegie Library of Pittsburgh.)

Three unidentified women working as pickle tasters at H. J. Heinz Company in 1905 are seen here in action. (Carnegie Library of Pittsburgh.)

Kenyon's Department Store (formerly Semple's) was located on Federal Street in Allegheny (now North Side). Thomas Kenyon (center) in the gray suit and derby is pictured with some of the clerks at the store around 1890. (Carnegie Library of Pittsburgh.)

This photograph shows the many faces of Pittsburgh glass factory workers—men, women, and children—in 1880. (Carnegie Library of Pittsburgh.)

Pig iron machines did not exist in 1880 when molten iron was cast from Pittsburgh's Eliza Blast Furnaces into molds in sand beds. The men were known as iron carriers, and their job was removing the pieces of pig iron from the sand. (Carnegie Library of Pittsburgh.)

A Muck Mill crew with their tools are photographed at the Pittsburgh Works prior to 1870. (Carnegie Library of Pittsburgh.)

This *c.* 1913 photograph shows men working at the Carnegie Painter Mill on Pittsburgh's South Side. (Carnegie Library of Pittsburgh.)

The many faces of the men of iron and steel can be seen in this photograph, taken of workers at an unidentified location in 1890. (Carnegie Library of Pittsburgh.)

The steel industry was crucial to Homestead, a borough situated on the left bank of the Monongahela River, just seven miles east of Pittsburgh. In the violent Homestead Strike, steel baron Andrew Carnegie and his partner Henry Clay Frick—known for his ruthless antiunion policy—with the help of hundreds of hired Pinkerton Agency detectives and the Pennsylvania State Militia, defeated the Amalgamated Association of Iron and Steel Workers. Three Pinkertons and seven workers died, and many more were wounded in the fight. The defeat of the workers halted the formation of unions in Pittsburgh steel companies until the 1930s. (Carnegie Library of Pittsburgh.)

Jones and Laughlin sales agents pose for a photograph at the entrance of the company's old general office and warehouse building in 1904. From left to right are (first row) H. F. Holloway from New York, F. H. Holt from Detroit, W. M. Kelly from Atlanta, George Kinsey from Cincinnati, Frank M. Campbell from Philadelphia, and William Armstrong from St. Louis; (second row) David N. Barker from Chicago, A. B. Marble from Boston, W. F. Bonnell from Cleveland, William Best Jr. from San Francisco, and George C. Beals from Buffalo. (Carnegie Library of Pittsburgh.)

A typical steelworker carefully places a piece of hot steel for processing on the job at the Homestead Steel Works around 1900. (Carnegie Library of Pittsburgh.)

The essence of iron and steel lies on the inside. This photograph gives a glimpse of the interior of a steel mill in the 1930s. (Carnegie Library of Pittsburgh.)

A little boy cleaning shoes on Conductor Street in April 1951 is shown in this photograph by Richard Saunders. (Carnegie Library of Pittsburgh.)

This photograph, taken in June 1950 in an unknown area of Pittsburgh, shows a solitary mill worker returning home from his job. (Carnegie Library of Pittsburgh.)

The work of the typical immigrant woman was never done. In this undated photograph, an unidentified woman washes clothes using two tubs and a manual wringer in front of a line of washing already hung to dry on her porch. (Carnegie Library of Pittsburgh.)

Many immigrants worked just as hard at home as they did at their jobs. In this photograph taken in the mid-1930s, John Alzo Sr. and his son John Jr. take a break from building a coal cellar at their Duquesne home. (Lisa A. Alzo.)

Banner bearing members of Local 1757 of the Congress of Industrial Organizations (CIO) steelworkers organizing committee are shown striding through Homestead in 1941. (Carnegie Library of Pittsburgh.)

Seven

AT PLAY

While most immigrants spent a majority of their waking hours working in the factories, mines, mills, or shops, on occasion men and women would take time for a bit of recreation or socialization with friends and neighbors. These interactions provided a reprieve from grueling jobs or mundane routines of daily life.

Amusement parks, festivals, and the big top circus provided entertainment for immigrants of all ages. Children met each other on the playgrounds. Adults interacted through church groups, ethnic clubs, or fraternal organizations and sports. Working people rarely met in each others' homes for social activities as the middle class did. Thus, bars, saloons, and neighborhood taverns served as a venue where men could have a drink and could visit with one another to share their complaints about company policy, discuss problems or politics, and play cards or other games to help them forget the drudgery of their everyday lives.

This poster (which now resides at the Western Pennsylvania Historical Society) shows the Eclipse Barge Club, organized in 1856 by amateur Pittsburgh oarsmen. The club's boats include *Eclipse*, *Darling*, *Albatross*, *Frolic*, and *Dembla*. Other boat clubs during this period were the Columbia, Oakmont, Undine, and Xanthe Boat Clubs. These clubs participated in both national and international races, but competition was abandoned in the 1890s because of betting corruption. (Carnegie Library of Pittsburgh.)

THE SCULL-RACE AT PITTSBURG—THE START FROM THE SUSPENSION BRIDGE.—[SKETCHED BY C. S. REINHART.]

Seen here is a drawing of the Scull Race between James Hamill of Pittsburgh and Walter Brown of Portland that brought 15,000 Pittsburghers to the river bank to watch the event in the rain on May 21, 1867. (Carnegie Library of Pittsburgh.)

The Iron City Fishing Club is captured in action by photographer Frank E. Bingaman around 1894. (Carnegie Library of Pittsburgh.)

Members of the Pittsburgh Golf Club, which was organized in 1896, are shown enjoying the day. The club's by-laws limited membership of the club to 500 members and stated that the insignia of the club "shall be a three-turreted tower, similar to that on the official seal of the City of Pittsburgh." (Carnegie Library of Pittsburgh.)

The Woman's Club of Pittsburgh, which resulted from Charles Dickens's second American visit in 1867, is the city's oldest club, and the ancestor of all women's clubs in the city and vicinity. The club is also the first federated club in Pennsylvania, and the second in the women's clubs. The name of the club and its program and members aroused harsh criticism of the press and the public. The Woman's Club of Pittsburgh pioneered in many advanced civic, educational, and cultural projects of Pittsburgh. In 1907, its members sponsored the State Convention for Equal Rights for Women held in the First Baptist Church on Fourth Avenue. Among the club's most famous members in 1887 was Elizabeth "Nellie Bly" Cochrane who later earned "round-the-world fame" (see page 49). (Carnegie Library of Pittsburgh.)

The Bohemian Club, founded in 1889, provided a social outlet for its members. This photograph features pianist Joseph Gittings, Maj. E. A. Montooth (leaning on piano), and Frank C. McGirr (third from left in rear, with pipe). (Carnegie Library of Pittsburgh.)

Two unidentified children hold onto a smaller child on a playground in Pittsburgh's Soho District around 1900. (Carnegie Library of Pittsburgh.)

This group of children posed outside in their coats and hats for this unidentified 1914 photograph. (Carnegie Library of Pittsburgh.)

Here is an example of a time when children did not need electronic games or gadgets for their entertainment. Two unidentified boys who are hiding, dressed in cowboy costumes, take aim behind some rocks in this undated photograph. (Carnegie Library of Pittsburgh.)

After all the fireworks and firecrackers have been shot off, then comes the task of gathering unexploded crackers, breaking them in the middle and making "fizzers" out of them, as these two young boys demonstrate in this 1912 photograph. (Carnegie Library of Pittsburgh.)

Kennywood Park began in 1898 as a picnic grove on Andrew Kenny's farm in Mifflin Township, and is now renowned for its world-famous roller coasters. Families, schools, and lodge and church groups flocked to this local amusement park in the spring and summer months to enjoy picnics, rides, and games. All the children liked Kennywood, and it was also nice for adults to spend an enjoyable afternoon under one of the shady oak or maple trees that were a trademark of the park. In this undated photograph, Verona Figlar holds her young daughter Margie during a day out at the park after a picnic basket lunch—typically ground up bologna mixed with sweet pickles and mayonnaise, and for dessert some bananas and cookies. (Lisa A. Alzo.)

Many changes occurred at the Kennywood Park between 1900 and 1930. In the early part of the second decade of the 20th century, Kennywood built two large roller coasters: the Racer and the Speed-O-Plane. Important rides added in the 1920s were three coasters; Jack Rabbit (designed by Miller and Baker in 1920), Pippin (designed by John Miller in 1924), and Racer in 1927, replacing the old Racer built in 1910. In this undated photograph, a group of nuns enjoy the thrill of a coaster ride. (Carnegie Library of Pittsburgh.)

Michael Sinchak (center) poses for a picture with two smiling, well-dressed ladies during Slovak Day at Kennywood Park in West Mifflin, Pennsylvania. Slovak Day, which was first held at the park in 1924, is one of several specially designated Nationality Days, which bring together Americans whose ancestors immigrated from around the world, to celebrate their heritage with a day of fun at Kennywood Amusement Park. (Teresa Sinchak.)

The Slovak Radio hour, "Vasa Nasa Slovenska Radiova Hodina," on WHJB, in 1938, featured live performances by local musicians. The show's host, Michael Sinchak (center), is pictured with one of the many bands that appeared live. Stanley Sinchak and Regina Feryok (née Sinchak) are shown in the background. (Teresa Sinchak.)

Sports such as basketball provided an outlet for recreation and socialization. This *c.* 1950 photograph shows the proud USA Local 1256 team of the U.S. Steel Plant in Duquesne, receiving a large trophy for their second place finish in the national USA championship. (Lisa A. Alzo.)

The first public swimming pool in the city was located on the South Side, along the banks of the Monongahela River. This photograph was taken by Frank Bingaman in 1908. (Carnegie Library of Pittsburgh.)

A good time was had by all whenever the circus came to town. This photograph shows a clown and other performers from a circus in the 1930s. (Carnegie Library of Pittsburgh.)

101

This photograph, which appeared in the *Pittsburgh-Sun Telegraph* in the Color-Gravure Section on April 27, 1930, shows a chorus of hardy steelworkers "practicing where there's lots of atmosphere." They seemed to find their inspiration in the upper stories of the Cathedral of Learning at the University of Pittsburgh as they prepared for the Pitt Cap and Gown show *Manhattan Preferred*. (Carnegie Library of Pittsburgh.)

Ethnic pride was shown by children, too. These children, in this unidentified photograph, gather together for a special event dressed in ornate costumes. (Carnegie Library of Pittsburgh.)

Will the real "St. Nick" please stand up? Members of the Syria Temple who played Santa Claus to thousands of orphans pose in this historical photograph. (Carnegie Library of Pittsburgh.)

After a hard day's work, enjoyment could be found in the simplest of pleasures. This undated photograph shows men drinking from a spilled keg of Fort Pitt beer on Second Avenue. (Carnegie Library of Pittsburgh.)

Workers in a typical mill town found their own means of entertainment. This c. 1900 photograph shows a group of men playing cards in a company-owned housing courtyard. (Carnegie Library of Pittsburgh.)

Eight

AT WORSHIP

From its inception, Pennsylvania's policy of religious tolerance has made it attractive to settlers from numerous religious denominations including Amish, Baptists, Episcopal, German Reformed, Greek Catholic, Jewish, Lutheran, Mennonite, Methodist, Moravian, Roman Catholic, and others.

Once immigrants settled in America, most fully embraced religious freedom and worked to build their own houses of worship. The immigrants who settled in the city of Pittsburgh and its surrounding neighborhoods were no different. In fact, in many neighborhoods, for example, there would be a Greek Catholic church on one corner, a Presbyterian church on another, and a Lutheran church down the road.

Pittsburgh is indeed a city of many religions. This fact is reflected in the following photographs of a few of the majestic cathedrals, exquisite churches and synagogues, and beautiful religious iconography that appear on the following pages.

Five miles east of Chicora, near Butler, stands an interesting old log edifice that was built in 1806—the first Catholic church west of the Allegheny Mountains (Saint Patrick's Log Church). The church was rededicated in 1926 by Bishop Hugh C. Boyle and used regularly for services. This photograph appeared in the *Pittsburgh Post-Gazette* on September 11, 1932. (Carnegie Library of Pittsburgh.)

Here is an example of how churches in Pittsburgh showed their strong ethnic identities. This photograph shows a sign in the window of a Slavic church at 1044 Spring Garden Avenue on Pittsburgh's North Side in July 1951. (Carnegie Library of Pittsburgh.)

The Shadyside Presbyterian Church stands tall above the trademark trees in this photograph snapped sometime between 1880 and 1882. One of the distinctive features of Shadyside Presbyterian Church's architecture is the "lantern" shape of its topmost roof. The structure is one of the finest examples of extant Richardsonian Romanesque Revival style. (Carnegie Library of Pittsburgh.)

This 1928 photograph shows the Congregation Beth Shalom, a Jewish synagogue in Squirrel Hill, before its new addition. (Carnegie Library of Pittsburgh.)

This undated photograph shows the Rodef Shalom temple at Eighth Street. Designed by Henry Hornbostel and dedicated in 1907, it was deemed, "One of the most beautiful and costly Jewish Synagogues in the United States." (Carnegie Library of Pittsburgh.)

The grand B'nai Israel Synagogue on North Negley Avenue is seen here. The original temple was designed for the B'nai Israel congregation in the mid-1920s by Henry Hornbostel (who also designed the Rodef Shalom temple). Set atop a grassy slope along a mostly residential Negley Avenue, the original temple has a massive stone rotunda with tall arched stained-glass windows. The main building is a three-tiered drum form with Roman arches and an entry porch, which has a vaulted ceiling constructed of Guastavino tiles. The main roof is a wood truss rotunda with a span of approximately 120 feet. (Carnegie Library of Pittsburgh.)

This is an undated illustration of the Unitarian Church on Pittsburgh's North Side that enjoys its own unique history. (Carnegie Library of Pittsburgh.)

Seen here is a sketch of the new East Liberty Presbyterian Church at the corner of Penn and Hiland Avenues, as it appeared in the *Pittsburgh Bulletin* on November 11, 1887. (Carnegie Library of Pittsburgh.)

St. Paul's Cathedral was consecrated on June 24, 1855, by Archbishop Hughes. It was on the site (Grant Street at Fifth Avenue) of the first cathedral, built in 1834, left atop a plateau by two "Hump" cuttings, and destroyed by fire in 1851. The cathedral was "acclaimed one of the finest church buildings in the U.S." (Carnegie Library of Pittsburgh.)

This photograph shows the fallen timbers amongst the ashes in St. Peter's Roman Catholic Church on Sarah Street destroyed by fire in 1952. (Carnegie Library of Pittsburgh.)

The beautiful structure of St. Agnes Roman Catholic Church, located at 3221 Fifth Avenue, is depicted in this undated photograph. (Carnegie Library of Pittsburgh.)

St. Augustine Church in Lawrenceville was founded in 1863 as a German ethnic parish, although the origin of the parish can actually be traced to the year 1854. This photograph was taken by University of Pittsburgh student Annette Lampe in the fall of 1978. The church merged with three others in 1993, and is now called Our Lady of the Angels Parish. (Carnegie Library of Pittsburgh.)

This nativity scene outside of St. Peter's Roman Catholic Church on Sarah Street reflects the holiness of the Christmas season. The convent behind the creche was demolished in 1997. (Carnegie Library of Pittsburgh.)

This undated image of a mural by Maximillen Vanka in St. Nicholas Croatian Roman Catholic Church in Millvale, Pennsylvania, reverently illustrates the theme of religion in the Old Country. (Carnegie Library of Pittsburgh.)

A 1903 architectural drawing from the
Pittsburgh Architectural Club exhibition
catalog, volume 3, depicts a grand
structure—a Greek Catholic Church in
Duquesne. (Carnegie Library
of Pittsburgh.)

The intricately designed altar and a few parishioners of St. John the Baptist Ukrainian Catholic
Church, located at 109 South Seventh Street, are captured in this undated photograph.
(Carnegie Library of Pittsburgh.)

This photograph of the Avery Institute African Methodist Episcopal Church on Pittsburgh's North Side was taken around 1938. (Carnegie Library of Pittsburgh.)

This is a photograph of the third East Liberty Presbyterian Church, once located at the corner of Penn and Highland Avenues. The church burned in 1888. (Carnegie Library of Pittsburgh.)

The Bellefield Presbyterian Church is grandly depicted in this undated photograph. Although the congregation was organized November 24, 1801, Bellefield Presbyterian Church has only been called by its present name since 1967, when two congregations were joined. Prior to this, the church family was known as First United Presbyterian Church of Pittsburgh for most of its history. (Carnegie Library of Pittsburgh.)

This undated photograph shows the front of the Duquesne Heights Baptist Church. Duquesne Heights and Mount Washington are located directly to the south of downtown Pittsburgh, and are surrounded by West End, Beechview, Beltzhoover, and Allentown. (Carnegie Library of Pittsburgh.)

Parishioners file out of St. Mary's Roman Catholic Church at Third and Ferry Streets in this 1950 photograph by Elliott Erwitt. (Carnegie Library of Pittsburgh.)

The Fourth Avenue Baptist Church was once on a portion of the site that is today occupied by the City-County Building. The present church, known as the First Baptist Church, is on Bellefield Avenue. (Carnegie Library of Pittsburgh.)

The Reverend James R. Cox (center in white robe) plays a character in the "St. Cecilia" play with other members of St. Mary's Church on Forty-sixth Street, in 1906, at Old Turner Hall on Forbes Street. Father Cox is most famous for his work with the unemployed during the Depression when he helped them build a slapdash city called Shantytown along Liberty Avenue. (Carnegie Library of Pittsburgh.)

This *c.* 1910 photograph, taken in old Chinatown along Second Avenue, shows a Chinese Altar ready for service. The image first appeared in the *Pittsburgh Sun-Telegraph* in the Color-Gravure Section on page 2, No. 9, on September 7, 1930. (Carnegie Library of Pittsburgh.)

Nine

MEMORABLE EVENTS

When one thinks of Pittsburgh, the image that most likely comes to mind is the large, smoky steel mill. Although once described as "Hell with the Lid Taken Off" by 19th century journalist James Parton in his article for the *Atlantic Monthly* in 1868, during the years following World War II, Pittsburgh was on the verge of big change.

Throughout the challenges that followed, many of Pittsburgh's prominent leaders remained poised to lead the city in a period of rebirth and renewal that would come to be known as the "Renaissance."

The book ends here with a few snapshots of some of the memorable events in the lives of many of Pittsburgh's immigrants.

This photograph, which shows a view of Sixth Avenue from Grant Street, was taken in 1908 during the celebration of Pittsburgh's 150th anniversary. (Carnegie Library of Pittsburgh.)

This photograph, titled *Celebrating Washington's Birthday*, appeared in the *Pittsburgh Sun-Telegraph* in the Color-Gravure Section on November 2, 1930. It shows members of the Women's Historical Society of Pennsylvania being entertained at the home of Amelia E. Rieck (middle of first row in the white dress) of Darlington Road in 1915. Other notable women in this picture include Minnie Ourey Roberts, founder of the Women's Club of Pittsburgh (third from left in the first row); Mrs. Edward A. Jones, president of the Women's Historical Society (fifth from right, first row); and Mrs. C. B. McFail, who succeeded her as president (second from right, first row). (Carnegie Library of Pittsburgh.)

Bertha Floersheim Rauh, wife of prominent Pittsburger Enoch Rauh and president of the Council of Jewish Women, brought the mayor of Indianapolis to Pittsburgh on March 27, 1912, to tell how he distributed potatoes to the poor of his hometown. This photograph captures that visit. From left to right are (first row) superintendent of police Martin J. Hyland of Indianapolis, Richard Rauh, Mrs. Shank, Bertha Rauh, and Mayor Samuel L. Shank of Indianapolis. Three unidentified gentleman make up the back row. (Carnegie Library of Pittsburgh.)

Photographer Frank Bingaman took this photograph, which shows a view of Market Street and Liberty Avenue in Pittsburgh during the St. Patrick's Day flood in 1936. (Carnegie Library of Pittsburgh.)

This photograph, taken by Harold Corsini in November 1950, shows an Oakland street during the "big snow." (Carnegie Library of Pittsburgh.)

Draftees leaving from Duquesne Wharf during World War I are shown in this 1917 photograph. (Carnegie Library of Pittsburgh.)

Hundreds of women drawn together with a common bond—a son serving in World War I—organized themselves as the Mothers of Democracy. This photograph shows them during an organized march. (Carnegie Library of Pittsburgh.)

During World War II, Pittsburgh was a key shipbuilding center. This LST-750 launched on Memorial Day 1944. The ship was financed by war bonds purchased by Allegheny County residents. (Carnegie Library of Pittsburgh.)

Dr. Frank Conrad, assistant chief engineer of Westinghouse Electric, first constructed a transmitter and installed it in a garage near his home in Wilkinsburg in 1916. The station was licensed as 8XK. At 6:00 p.m. on November 2, 1920, 8KX became KDKA Radio, and began broadcasting, with the returns for the Harding-Cox presidential election, at 100 watts from a makeshift shack atop one of the Westinghouse manufacturing buildings in east Pittsburgh. (Carnegie Library of Pittsburgh.)

This photograph shows one of 26 nationality classrooms constructed within the Cathedral of Learning at the University of Pittsburgh between 1938 and 1999. According to the university, each classroom represents a different cultural heritage; from Poland to Russia, China to Italy, India to England, each classroom demonstrates the beauty and heritage of a particular country—and the intercultural ties that the descendents of those cultures, now living in America, continue to cherish. Among the documents placed in the Cathedral of Learning cornerstone, set in 1937, is a copper plate engraved with these thoughts expressed by the Nationality Room Committee chairpersons to the university: "Faith and peace are in their hearts. Good will has brought them together. Like the Magi of ancestral traditions and the shepherds of candid simplicity, they offer their gifts of what is precious, genuine and their own, to truth that shines forever and enlightens all people." (Carnegie Library of Pittsburgh.)

Throughout its history, Pittsburgh, the greatest U.S. industrial city of the 19th century, saw its share of both big highs and lows. In response, business and political leaders, led by banker Richard King Mellon and Mayor David L. Lawrence in 1945, launched what became known as the Pittsburgh Renaissance, a unique attempt to renew a major industrial city that lasted until 1969. The Renaissance was the product of a new type of partnership that combined public authority with private funding. It was directed by the Allegheny Conference on Community Development, a nonprofit committee with the city's most powerful business leaders as members. The goals of the Pittsburgh Renaissance were environmental improvement (controlling smoke pollution and floods and treating sewage), downtown renewal, and transportation revitalization. This photograph, taken by Harold Corsini in August 1952, shows a view of downtown Pittsburgh, and its famed "Point." (Carnegie Library of Pittsburgh.)

BIBLIOGRAPHY

Burns, Daniel J. *Duquesne*. Charleston, SC: Arcadia Publishing, 2005.

Davenport, Marcia. *The Valley of Decision*. New York City: Charles Scribner's Sons, 1943.

Lorant, Stefan. *Pittsburgh: The Story of an American City*, 4th ed. Lenox, MA: Author Edition, Inc., 1988.

Parton, James. "Pittsburg." *Atlantic Monthly*, January 21, 1868.

Standiford, Les. *Meet You in Hell: Andrew Carnegie, Henry Clay Frick and the Bitter Partnership that Transformed America*. New York City: Crown Publishing Group, a Division of Random House, Inc., 2005.

The Squirrel Hill Historical Society. *Squirrel Hill*. Charleston, SC: Arcadia Publishing, 2005.

Yardley, Jonathan. *States of Mind: A Personal Journey Through the Mid Atlantic*. New York City: Villard Books, 1993.

DISCOVER THOUSANDS OF LOCAL HISTORY BOOKS
FEATURING MILLIONS OF VINTAGE IMAGES

Arcadia Publishing, the leading local history publisher in the United States, is committed to making history accessible and meaningful through publishing books that celebrate and preserve the heritage of America's people and places.

Find more books like this at
www.arcadiapublishing.com

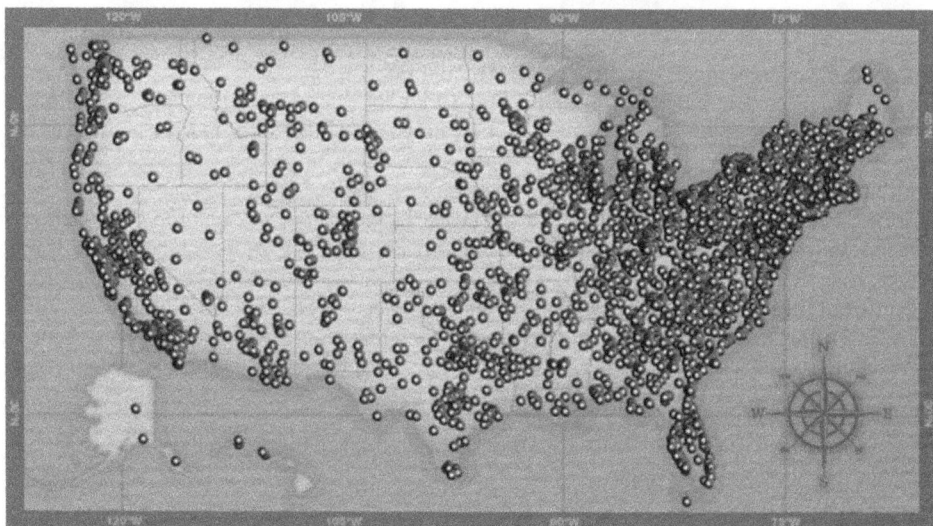

Search for your hometown history, your old stomping grounds, and even your favorite sports team.

Consistent with our mission to preserve history on a local level, this book was printed in South Carolina on American-made paper and manufactured entirely in the United States. Products carrying the accredited Forest Stewardship Council (FSC) label are printed on 100 percent FSC-certified paper.

MADE IN THE USA

www.ingramcontent.com/pod-product-compliance
Lightning Source LLC
Chambersburg PA
CBHW050655150426
42813CB00055B/2194